D0122293

THE ZEN
OF SMALL THINGS

Stephanie JT Russell

Ariel Books

**Andrews McMeel
Publishing**
Kansas City

Photos by Stephanie JT Russell

06 07 08 09 10 TWP 10 9 8 7 6 5 4 3 2 1

ISBN-13: 978-0-7407-5729-7
ISBN-10: 0-7407-5729-6

Library of Congress Control Number: 2005928877

For Isaac and Leah

Not the endpoint

but the stations between.

Not the thing unheard

but the one hearing it.

———

Not conception,

but the instant before birth.

Neither day's end

nor night's beginning.

Neither dream nor sleep,

nor waking even again.

—

And who's to say that a shadow doesn't whisper,

or that river stones don't sing?

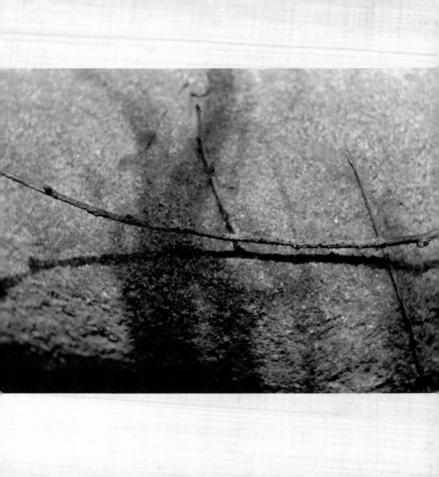

Your hands in the dirt are a
poem. Their latent purpose
is a product unto itself.
They are the master builder
of a utopia made in the soil
of change.

———

Not the pond,

but the reflection.

Not reflection,

but the thing contained in it.

———

Not the container,

but the emptiness it holds.

Not emptiness,

but pure potential filling its

boundless margins.

———

The germ of idea, seeking

its place in the timeless dusk of

infinite possibility.

———

Not life but the things left behind:

a child's ball on the pavement, the

chip in a teacup, the spine of a

well-loved book.

—

Neither water itself nor the

hand lifting to drink.

And the moon's vivid emptiness when

it's invisible to the eye.

—

Not the blemished self, but its native perfection.

Not perfection, but the stainless grace of humility.

Not humility, but the subtle poise of surrender.

Not surrender, but the thing that leads one to it.

—

Neither leading nor

following. Not arriving, ever.

—

Not silence, but the attention

needed to hear it.

Not attention, but the silence

that calls one to it.

——

Not the riverbank, but
seasons changing upon it.
Not the tree, but its
unexpected appearance in
the thicket.

—

Seeing the world as if it's being

created before your eyes. Like a

dreaming child who might never

return from wonder.

Not the highest ideal, but the
lowliest everyday custom.
Not everyday custom, but its
unutterable hidden mystery.
Not mystery, but its promise
to remain unseen.

———

A child sees himself in everything. In his mind, it is how things are, and how he imagines they will always be. Later, as a man, he forgets it, when being right seems more important than being loved. Till finally he stills his mind and glimpses himself in the rain, the sea, a patch of soil, a stranger in the street, younger than he's ever been before.

——

Not the observer, but the
thing observed. Not the
thing observed, but its place
within the whole.

———

Not the whole, but its position

within the moment.

Not the moment, but the

observer within it.

Not the observer, but the

rapture of pure observation.

———

Paying attention is an art

form. It distinguishes love

from mere appetite. And

loving things as they are,

rather than as we wish them

to be: one small thing that

keeps the world from

spinning off its axis.

———

When the lustre of mundane detail

touches the spirit with soundless ecstasy.

—

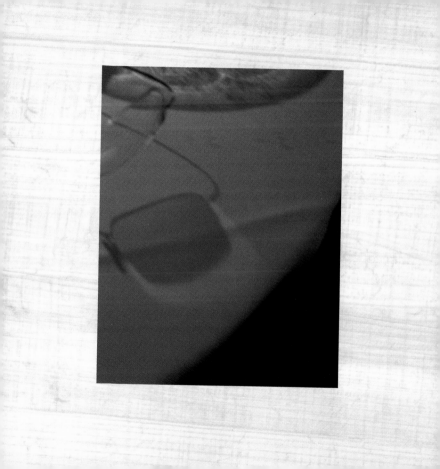

Not the plum, but the branch

that holds it.

Not the branch, but the

broom it makes later.

———

Not sweeping floors,

but waiting for dust to gather.

Not dust,

but the action that creates it.

Not action, nor creating.

Nor expecting anything to occur.

———

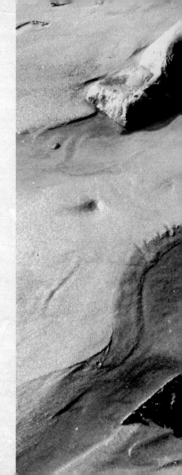

Neither false assurances

nor childish hopes,

but the precise, raw

truth of now.

—

Awakening is the physics of
desire, unexpectedly fulfilled.
A silent storm of lucidity
flooding in from the dark.

———

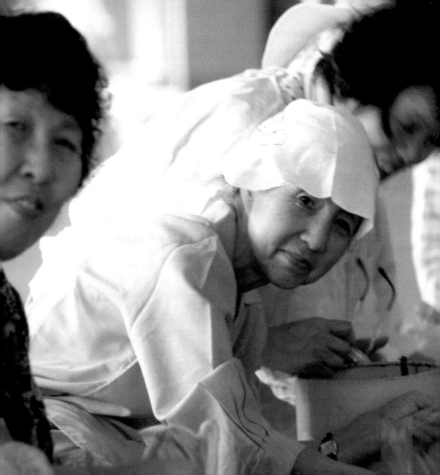

The unclouded eye, cleaving

to the thing not understood,

not yet known, not yet seen.

—

The strand of the original self lies in the essence of small things. In the eyes of a solitary traveler on the bus. In the grain of old wood beaten softly by the years. In the heft of a tool that has served someone well. You are in everything that you see and do not see.

——

Everything you see, and everything
you do not see, abiding in a future self
you have yet to meet.

—

Everything you see and do not see, living in the present self, in each of the ten one thousand universes you now occupy.

—

The elemental, original self,

caught for a fleeting instant in

a simple bead of rain. As in

each of the ten one thousand

universes now containing you.

—

As in the ten one thousand

sorrows and joys you know.

Each crowded with infinite

detail, all deep in your bones

unaware.

———

As in each of the ten one thousand

memories gathered in your every step.

Evanescent as the ten one thousand

things you touch, smell, and see as the

day slips by barely noticed.

———

And the memory of places

you have never visited till now.

—

In the endless ocean of change, each
drop becoming a wave, each wave
becoming the next. As each moment
becomes the next, and disappears in
the becoming.

———

As in the light, most useful for the

shadow it creates. As in shadow, most

useful for its power to evoke.

———

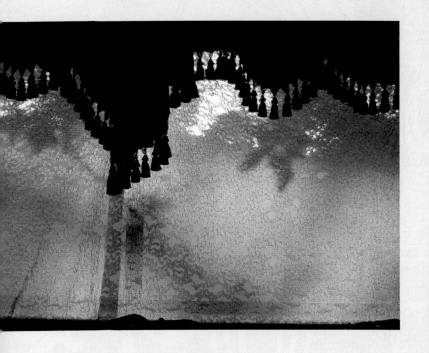

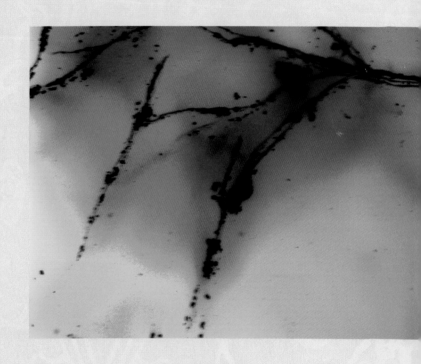

As in emptiness, the

transparent vessel of spirit

through which everything

must pass.

——

In only the empty vessel can the

smallest thing be contained.

———

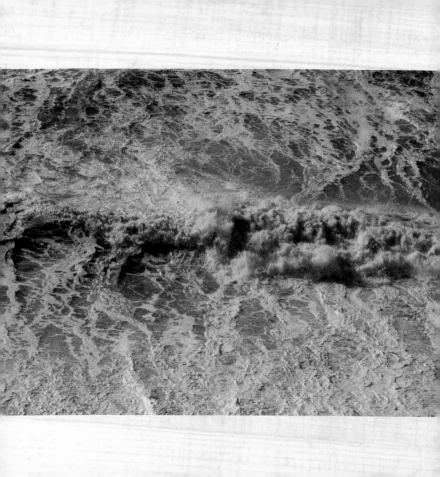

This book is set in Bembo, Tagliente, and Trajan

Designed by Junie Lee Tait

in New York City

—